Catholic
Prayer Book

Prayer Book of Catholic Prayers

Catholic Youth Prayer Book

By : Gala Publication

Published By :

Gala Publication

Table of Contents

My Daily Prayer

O My God,
I place my trust and confidence in You,
who will reward the good and punish the wicked.
I believe in You and accept everything
You have taught and revealed.

I believe that in one God
there are three Divine Persons -
God the Father,
God the Son
and God the Holy Spirit.

I believe that God the Son became Man
without ceasing to be God.
He is Jesus Christ, my lord and my Saviour,
the Redeemer of the human race.
He died on the Cross for my salvation
and eternal happiness.

O my God, give me a strong faith.
Help me to believe with lively faith.

O my God, all-good and all-merciful,
I sincerely hope to be saved.
Help me to do all that is necessary
to gain eternal salvation.

I have committed many sins in my life,
but now I turn away from them.
I am sorry, truly sorry for all of them,
because I have offended You, my God,
Who are all-good, all-perfect,
all-holy and all-merciful.

I love you, O my God, with all my heart.
Please forgive me for having offended You.

I promise that, with Your help,
I will never offend You again.

My God, have mercy on me.

Morning and Evening Prayers

Morning Offering

My God, I offer you my prayers,
works, joys and sufferings of this day
in union with the holy sacrifice of the Mass
throughout the world.
I offer them for all the intentions of your Son's
Sacred Heart,
for the salvation of souls, reparation for sin,
and the reunion of Christians.

Morning Prayer

God, our Father, I offer you today
all that I think and do and say.
I offer it with what was done
on earth by Jesus Christ, your Son.

Evening Prayer

God, our Father, this day is done.
We ask you and Jesus Christ, your Son,
that with the Spirit, our welcome guest,
you guard our sleep and bless our rest.

Night Prayer

God, come to my assistance.
Lord make haste to help me.
Glory be to the Father,
and to the Son,
and the Holy Spirit;
as it was in the beginning,
is now and ever shall be,
world without end.
O my God, I thank you for having preserved me
today
and for having given me so many blessings and
graces.
I renew my dedication to you and ask your pardon
for all my sins.

Mealtime Prayers

Prayer Before Meals

Bless us, O Lord, and these your gifts
which we are about to receive from your goodness.
Through Christ our Lord.

Prayer After Meals

We give you thanks
for all your gifts,
almighty God,
living and reigning
now and for ever.

Everyday Prayer

Jesus, I entrust all my problems to you.
Come to me.
Speak to me.
Reveal the will of God to me.
Deliver me from dangers and diseases (names).
Jesus! Pour your precious blood on me.
Remove all the stain of sin from me.
Grant me freely, redemption from sin
and salvation by the merit of the crucifixion
and glorious resurrection of Jesus Christ.
Deliver me from satanic bondages,
evil desire, wicked men
and temptations of the devil.
Save me by the merit of your suffering.
Jesus, send upon me, in power,
the Holy Spirit,
promised by the Father.
Renew me,
and my dear ones by the Holy Spirit.
Thank you God.
Praise be Jesus.
Praise be the Holy Spirit."

Prayers Every Catholic Should Know

Act of Contrition

My God,
I am sorry for my sins with all my heart.
In choosing to do wrong
and failing to do good,
I have sinned against you
whom I should love above all things.
I firmly intend, with your help,
to do penance,
to sin no more,
and to avoid whatever leads me to sin.
Our Savior Jesus Christ
suffered and died for us.
In his name, my God, have mercy.

Act of Faith

O my God, I firmly believe that you are one God in
three divine Persons, Father, Son, and Holy Spirit. I
believe that your divine Son became man and died for
our sins, and that he will come to judge the living and
the dead. I believe these and all the truths which the
holy Catholic Church teaches, because you have revealed

them, who can neither deceive nor be deceived.

Act of Hope

O my God, relying on your infinite mercy and promises, I
hope to obtain pardon of my sins, the help of your grace,
and life everlasting, through the merits of Jesus Christ,
my Lord and Redeemer

Act of Love

O my God, I love you above all things with my whole
heart and soul, because you are all good and worthy of all
my love. I love my neighbor as myself for the love of
you. I forgive all who have injured me and I ask pardon
of those whom I have injured.

Apostles' Creed

I believe in God,
the Father almighty,
Creator of heaven and earth,
and in Jesus Christ, his only Son, our Lord,
who was conceived by the Holy Spirit,
born of the Virgin Mary,
suffered under Pontius Pilate,
was crucified, died and was buried;
he descended into hell;
on the third day he rose again from the dead;

he ascended into heaven,

and is seated at the right hand of God the Father
almighty;
from there he will come to judge the living and the dead.
I believe in the Holy Spirit,
the holy catholic Church,
the communion of saints,
the forgiveness of sins,
the resurrection of the body,
and life everlasting.

Lord's Prayer

Our Father,
who art in heaven,
hallowed be thy name;
thy kingdom come;
thy will be done
on earth as it is in heaven.
Give us this day our daily bread;
and forgive us our trespasses
as we forgive those who trespass against us;
and lead us not into temptation,
but deliver us from evil.

Hail Holy Queen

Hail, Holy Queen, Mother of mercy, our life, our
sweetness, and our hope. To thee do we cry, poor
banished children of Eve. To thee do we send up our
sighs, mourning and weeping in this vale of tears. Turn
then, most gracious advocate, thine eyes of mercy
towards us and after this, our exile, show unto us the
blessed fruit of thy womb, Jesus. O clement, O loving, O
sweet Virgin Mary. V. Pray for us, O holy Mother of
God. R. That we may be made worthy of the promises of
Christ.

Prayer After Mass

Anima Christi
Soul of Christ, make me holy. Body of Christ, save me.
Blood of Christ, fill me with love. Water from Christ's
side, wash me. Passion of Christ, strengthen me. Good
Jesus, hear me. Within your wounds, hide me. Never let
me be parted from you. From the evil enemy, protect me.
At the hour of my death, call me, and tell me to come to
you that with your saints I may praise you through all
eternity.

Prayers to the Holy Spirit

Prayer to the Holy Spirit
Breathe into me Holy Spirit, that all my thoughts may be
holy. Move in me, Holy Spirit, that my work, too, may be
holy. Attract my heart, Holy Spirit, that I may love only
what is holy. Strengthen me, Holy Spirit, that I may
defend all that is holy. Protect me, Holy Spirit, that I
always may be holy.
Come, Holy Spirit
Come, O Holy Spirit, fill the hearts of your faithful and
enkindle in them the fire of your love. Send forth your
Spirit, and they shall be created. And you shall renew the
face of the earth.
Let us pray
O God, who has taught the hearts of the faithful by the
light of the Holy Spirit, grant that by the gift of the same

Spirit we may be always truly wise and ever rejoice in his consolation, through Christ our Lord.

Prayer To Saint Michael The Archangel

O glorious prince St. Michael,
  chief and commander of the heavenly hosts,
  guardian of souls, vanquisher of rebel spirits,
servant in the house of the Divine King
and our admirable conductor,
  you who shine with excellence
and superhuman virtue deliver us from all evil
who turn to you with confidence
and enable us by your gracious protection
  to serve God more and more faithfully every day.

Prayer To Your Guardian Angel

Angel of God,
my guardian dear,
To whom God's love
commits me here,
Ever this day,
be at my side,
To light and guard,
Rule and guide.

Children's Prayer To Mary

Dear Mother of Jesus,
look down upon me
As I say my prayers slowly
at my mother's knee.

I love thee, O Lady
and please willest thou bring
All little children
To Jesus our King.

Prayer To Our Lady, Help Of Christians

Most Holy Virgin Mary, Help of Christian,
how sweet it is to come to your feet
imploring your perpetual help.
If earthly mothers cease not to remember their
children,

how can you, the most loving of all mothers forget
me?
Grant then to me, I implore you,
your perpetual help in all my necessities,
in every sorrow, and especially in all my temptations.
I ask for your unceasing help for all who are now
suffering.

Help the weak, cure the sick, convert sinners.
Grant through your intercessions many vocations to
the religious life.
Obtain for us, O Mary, Help of Christians,
that having invoked you on earth we may love and
eternally thank you in heaven.

Thirty Days' Prayer to Saint Joseph

Ever blessed and glorious Joseph, kind and loving father, and helpful friend of all in sorrow! You are the good father and protector of orphans, the defender of the defenseless, the patron of those in need and sorrow. Look kindly on my request. My sins have drawn down on me the just displeasure of my God, and so I am surrounded with unhappiness. To you, loving guardian of the Family of Nazareth, do I go for help and protection.

Listen, then, I beg you, with fatherly concern, to my earnest prayers, and obtain for me the favors I ask.

I ask it by the infinite mercy of the eternal Son of God, which moved Him to take our nature and to be born into this world of sorrow.

I ask it by the weariness and suffering you endured when you found no shelter at the inn of Bethlehem for the holy Virgin, nor a house where the Son of God could be born. Then, being everywhere refused, you had to allow the Queen of Heaven to give birth to the world's Redeemer in a cave.

I ask it by that painful torture you felt at the prophecy of holy Simeon, which declared the Child Jesus and His holy Mother future victims of our sins and of their great love for us.

I ask it through your sorrow and pain of soul when the angel declared to you that the life of the Child Jesus was sought by His enemies. From their evil plan you had to flee with Him and His Blessed Mother to Egypt. I ask it by all the suffering, weariness, and labors of that long and dangerous journey.

I ask it by all your care to protect the Sacred Child and His Immaculate Mother during your second journey, when you were ordered to return to your own country. I ask it by your peaceful life in Nazareth where you met with so many joys and sorrows.

I ask it by your great distress when the adorable Child was lost to you and His Mother for three days. I ask it by your joy at finding Him in the Temple, and by the comfort you found at Nazareth, while living in the company of the Child Jesus. I ask it by the wonderful submission He showed in His obedience to you.

I ask it by the perfect love and conformity you showed in accepting the Divine order to depart from this life, and from the company of Jesus and Mary. I ask it by the joy which filled your soul, when the Redeemer of the world, triumphant over death and hell, entered into the possession of His kingdom and led you into it with special honors.

I ask it through Mary's glorious Assumption, and through that endless happiness you have with her in the presence of God.

O good father! I beg you, by all your sufferings, sorrows, and joys, to hear me and obtain for me what I ask.

Obtain for all those who have asked my prayers everything that is useful to them in the plan of God. Finally, my dear patron and father, be with me and all who are dear to me in our last moments, that we may eternally sing the praises of Jesus, Mary and Joseph.

A Prayer To My Lord

My Lord,
I offer you my thoughts:
to be fixed on you;
My words:
to have you for their theme;
My actions:
to reflect my love for you;
My sufferings:
to be endured for your greater glory.
I want to do what you ask of me:
In the way you ask,
For as long as you ask,
Because you ask it.
Lord, enlighten my understanding,
Strengthen my will,
Purify my heart,
and make me holy.
Help me to repent of my past sins
And to resist temptation in the future.
Help me to rise above my human weaknesses

And to grow stronger as a Christian.

A Spirit To Know You

Gracious and Holy Father,
Please give me:
intellect to understand you,
reason to discern you,
diligence to seek you,
wisdom to find you,
a spirit to know you,
a heart to meditate upon you,
ears to hear you,
eyes to to see you,
a tongue to proclaim you,
a way of life pleasing to you,
patience to wait for you
and perseverance to look for you.
Grant me a perfect end,
your holy presence,
a blessed resurrection
and life everlasting.

Act Of Humility After Holy Communion

O Jesus, my God!
Thou art infinite in all perfections;
and I am but dust,

and unto dust shall I return.
Depart from me, O Lord,
for I am a sinful man.
Yet, O my sweet Jesus,
if Thou leavest me,
to whom shall I go?
What will become of me?
Rather will I say,
"Stay with me, Lord;
abide always within my heart;
and may my heart make ever sacrifice for Thee.".

Act Of Oblation Before Holy Mass

Eternal Father,
I offer Thee the sacrifice wherein Thy dear Son Jesus
offered Himself upon the Cross
and which He now renews upon this altar,
to adore Thee and to render to Thee that honour
which is Thy due,
acknowledging Thy supreme dominion over all
things
and their absolute dependence on Thee,
for Thou art our first beginning and our last end;
to give Thee thanks for countless benefits received;
to appease Thy justice provoked to anger by so many
sins,
and to offer Thee worthy satisfaction for the same;
and finally to implore Thy grace and mercy for

myself,
for all those who are in tribulation and distress,
for all poor sinners,
for the whole world
and for the blessed souls in purgatory.

Air Force Prayer

Lord guard and guide the men who fly,
Through the great spaces of sky.
Be with them as they take to air,
Im morning light and sunshine fair.
Eternal Father, strong to save,
Give them courage, make them brave;
Protect them whereso'er they go,
From shell and flak and fire and foe.
Most loved Member of their crew,
Ride with them up in the blue.
Direct their bombs upon the foe,
but shelter those whom Thou dost know.
Keep them together upon their way.
Grant their work success today.
Deliver them from hate and sin,
and bring them safely down again.
O God bless the men who fly,
Through lonely way across the sky,

Prayer For A Loved One's Conversion

O Father, in the name of Your Son Jesus,
and in the power and authority of the Holy Spirit,
I ask that You fill [name]
with the knowledge of Your will
through all spiritual wisdom and understanding.
Enlighten this precious child of Yours, dear Lord!
Teach this dear one to live in a manner
that is worthy of You,
so as to be fully pleasing to You,
full of good works bearing good fruits
and ever growing in knowledge of You.
Strengthen this lost lamb, dear Lord,
with every power of Your Holy Spirit,
in accordance with Your might,
for all endurance and patience,
with joy, giving thanks to You O Father!
Make Your child fit to share in the inheritance
of the holy ones in the Light.
Deliver this beloved one from the power of darkness
and transfer [name]
into the kingdom of Your Beloved Son, Jesus,
in whom is redemption and the forgiveness of sins.

The Prayer, Dear Lord Jesus.

Dear Lord Jesus,
May we stand before you in our brokenness,
our weakness and our fragile humanity.
We are sorrowful for all the times we've
disappointed you.
We pray that the next time we are tempted to gossip,
to accuse, to judge or to despise another,
we may instead be strengthened with the Grace of
the Holy Spirit
to speak words of godliness and to act with Charity.
May Love be the motive for every decision we
choose in our lives.

Litany of the Sacred Passion

The Litany of the Sacred Passion may be used in
conjunction with the "Seven Last Words" or as a
separate devotion. It draws together all the events of
Jesus' dying day.
Lord Jesus, at the Last Supper you knew that Judas,
one of the Twelve, would betray you.
~GOOD LORD, DELIVER US FROM FALSE
FRIENDS AND TREACHERY.
Lord Jesus, during the supper, you humbly washed
the feet of your disciples.
~GOOD LORD, MAKE US MEEK AND

HUMBLE OF HEART.

Lord Jesus, at the Last Supper, you gave us the sacrament of your broken body and outpoured blood.

~GOOD LORD, WE WORSHIP THE SEAL OF THE NEW AND ETERNAL COVENANT.

Lord Jesus, you asked your disciples to watch and pray with you in the Garden of Gethsemane.

~GOOD LORD, KEEP US AWAKE AND WATCHFUL WITH YOU.

Lord Jesus, at your betrayal and arrest all your friends fled in fear and deserted you.

~GOOD LORD, GIVE US COURAGE IN TIME OF TRIAL.

Lord Jesus, you were falsely accused and condemned for speaking the truth before Caiaphas, the high priest.

~GOOD LORD, MAY WE SPEAK TRUTH IN THE FACE OF INJUSTICE.

Lord Jesus, in the courtyard of the high priest, Simon Peter swore three times that he did not know you.

~GOOD LORD, MAKE US FAITHFUL IN TIME OF TEMPTATION.

Lord Jesus, Pilate traded you for a murderer and handed you over to crucifixion.

~GOOD LORD, HAVE MERCY ON US SINNERS.

Lord Jesus, you were beaten, mocked, and
humiliated by Pilate's soldiers.
~GOOD LORD, MAY WE SUFFER GLADLY
FOR YOUR SAKE.
Lord Jesus, on the cross you were taunted and
derided as King of the Jews.
~GOOD LORD, MAY WE ALWAYS LIVE IN
OBEDIENCE TO YOU.
Lord Jesus, on the cross you forgave your enemies.
~GOOD LORD, GIVE US THE GRACE TO
FORGIVE OURS.

Lord Jesus, from the cross you promised paradise to
a repentant criminal.
~GOOD LORD, MAKE US LONG FOR
PARADISE AND ETERNAL BLISS.
Lord Jesus, from the cross you confided your
Blessed Mother to your beloved disciple.
~GOOD LORD, MAKE US CHILDREN OF
MARY.
Lord Jesus, you cried out in agony to your Father
and died with a loud cry.
~GOOD LORD, HAVE MERCY ON US, NOW
AND AT THE HOUR OF OUR DEATH.
Lord Jesus, the Roman centurion recognized you as
the Son of God.
~GOOD LORD, MAY WE ALWAYS PRAISE
AND EXALT YOU AS OUR BLESSED SAVIOR.
Lord Jesus, you were taken down from the cross and

laid in the arms of your sorrowful Mother.

~GOOD LORD, ENTRUST US TO THE CARE
OF YOUR BLESSED MOTHER.

Lord Jesus, Joseph of Arimathea wrapped your body
in a linen shroud and laid you in his rock-hewn
tomb.

~GOOD LORD, GRANT US THE GIFT OF
TEARS AT THE MEMORY OF YOUR
SUFFERING, DEATH, AND BURIAL.

Lord Jesus, the women who had followed you from
Galilee watched as you were put to rest in the tomb.

~GOOD LORD, WE AWAIT WITH JOY YOUR
GLORIOUS RESURRECTION ON THE THIRD
DAY.

(Pause for special intentions.)

We adore you, O Christ, and we bless you,

~FOR BY YOUR HOLY CROSS YOU HAVE
REDEEMED THE WORLD.

Easter Acts Of Consecration

To be prayed at the beginning of each prayer below:
Leader: Let us commend ourselves and all people
    to the love and protection of the Mother of God.
All: Holy Mother of God, Mary ever Virgin,
    intercede for us with the Lord our God.
Leader: God who is mighty has done great things for us.
All: And holy is God's name.
Leader: Let us pray:

Sunday

Mary,
On this, the Lord's Day,
We celebrate with joy the fulfillment of the miracle
God began in your womb.
He became what we are
So that we might become what he is.
He is Risen, the first-fruits of those who have fallen asleep.
He reigns as Lord and God forever.
In your marveling at the great things the Mighty One worked in you,
We find our own awe at being chosen sons (and daughters) of God,

Of being empowered to become a nation of saints,
Of being commissioned to bear Christ to the world.
With you as our companion and model,
May God bring this good work to completion
And may our dedication to you of all that we have
and are
Bring us to share in your blessedness.

Monday

Mary,
God has worked a great wonder: Jesus is risen!
No longer are we caught in the cords of death,
For he has loosened our bonds.
No longer need we walk in fear,
For he has become our strong hope.
No longer are we alone and estranged,
For he has called us friends.
May your faith in the face of death - even death on
the cross,
May your hope - almost buried with him in the
tomb,
May your love - nearly staunched by the fear of his
disciples,
May your joy in the Resurrected Savior be ours this
day,
As we, in your name for your honor, live out our
Easter mission
To go forth and teach all peoples.

Tuesday

Mary,
We, your sons (and daughters)
Look to you as we treasure and ponder
The Rising of Jesus - your Son and our brother.
Teach us how that marvelous moment can topple
the proud,
Elevate the lowly, feed the hungry,
And mission the rich - even today.
Confident in God's power and love,
Trusting in the Risen Lord,
Relying on the Promised Advocate,
The Spirit of Life and of Truth,
We dedicate our lives, in your name and for your
honor
To the transforming power of Easter.

Wednesday

Mary,
In the brilliant light of Easter,
Teach us, too, that nothing is impossible with God.
All our struggles with self and others,
All our disappointments and shames,
All our failures and sinfulness
Are as nothing in this healing, life-giving light.
Accept, then, our all.
May God look upon it,

As once did the Mighty One upon our lowliness,
So that we might be gifted with that blessedness
Promised to all sons and daughters of the
Resurrection.

Thursday

Mary,
We sing our Alleluias today, for Jesus is risen.
Our souls proclaim the greatness of God,
Our spirits rejoice in our Risen Savior.
May your song be sung in our lives
At every moment of this day so that God's power,
Which can do far more than we can ask or imagine,
May continue to call life from death and light from
darkness,
Transforming our meager efforts
Into your Son's victory over death.

Friday

Mary,
The cross of death has become the Tree of Life, and
we rejoice.
God has sent forth the Spirit,
And the world quickens to life anew.
Jesus is risen!
Teach us no more to fear the sword of division and
death;

Teach us to welcome Jesus, the sign of contradiction,
And to lay bare the thoughts of our hearts
To the healing light of Easter.
Then, in your name and for your honor,
We will live in the Paschal Mystery
Today and, with you, see it fulfilled
On the day of Resurrection.

Saturday

Mary,
We ask for your powerful presence this day,
Just as you shared it
With the frightened disciples in the Upper Room.
Teach us, as you did them, to rely upon God's promises,
Upon our brother and Lord, Jesus, and
Upon the Advocate and Comforter,
The Spirit of Life and Love and Truth.
May we live as you did, in strong hope and invicible confidence.
And be transformed by the power of the Resurrection
Into true hearers and doers of God's will.

Prayer For Faith

Lord, I believe:
I wish to believe in Thee.
Lord, let my faith be full and unreserved,
and let it penetrate my thought,
my way of judging Divine things and human things.
Lord, let my faith be joyful
and give peace and gladness to my spirit,
and dispose it for prayer with God
and conversation with men,
so that the inner bliss of its fortunate possession
may shine forth in sacred and secular conversation.
Lord, let my faith be humble and not presume
to be based on the experience of my thought and of
my feeling;
but let it surrender to the testimony of the Holy
Spirit,
and not have any better guarantee than in docility to
Tradition
and to the authority of the magisterium of the Holy
Church.

Good Friday Prayer

O Jesus, Who by reason of Thy burning love for us
hast willed to be crucified
and to shed Thy Most Precious Blood
for the redemption and salvation of our souls,
look down upon us here gathered together
in remembrance of Thy most sorrowful Passion and
Death,
fully trusting in Thy mercy;
cleanse us from sin by Thy grace,
sanctify our toil,
give unto us and unto all those who are dear to us
our daily bread,
sweeten our sufferings,
bless our families,
and to the nations so sorely afflicted,
grant Thy peace,
which is the only true peace,
so that by obeying Thy commandments
we may come at last to the glory of heaven.

Prayer To The Heart Of Jesus

O Jesus, we know you are gentle
and that you gave your Heart for us.
It was crowned with thorns through our sins.
We know that even today you are praying for us
so that we will not be lost.

Jesus, remember us when we fall into sin.

Through your most Sacred Heart,
make us all love one another.
Cause hatred to disappear among men.
Show us your love.
We all love you
and we want you to protect us
with your Heart of the Good Shepherd.
Come into each heart, Jesus!
Knock at the door of our hearts.
Be patient and persistent with us.
We are still closed up in ourselves
because we have not understood your will.
Knock continuously, O Jesus,
make our hearts open to you,
at least in remembering the Passion you have
suffered for us.

Heart Prayer

Saint Michael,
your heart was filled with great charity
for God and man.
Our Lord returned your love
and allowed you to exchange mystically
your heart with His.
Pray for all whose hearts
are afflicted with illness, fear, or loneliness.

Teach us to be resigned to God's will
in all the trials and sicknesses.
Help us to live as you lived -
to do good now and for eternity.

Prayer To Jesus Christ, Lord

Jesus Christ, Lord of all things,
You see my heart;
You know my desires.
Possess all that I am, You alone.
I am Your sheep;
make me worthy to overcome the devil.

Prayers After Confession

My dearest Jesus,
I have told all my sins to the best of my ability.
I have sincerely tried to make a good confession
and I know that you have forgiven me.
Thank you dear Jesus!
Your divine heart is full of love and mercy for poor
sinners.
I love You dear Jesus;
you are so good to me.
My loving Saviour,
I shall try to keep from sin
and to love You more each day.

Dearest Mother Mary,
pray for me and help me to keep all my promises.
Protect me and do not let me fall back into sin.
Dear God,
help me to lead a good life.
Without Your grace I can do nothing.

Act Of Contrition

My God,
I am sorry for my sins with all my heart.
In choosing to do wrong
and failing to do good,
I have sinned against you
whom I should love above all things.
I firmly intend, with your help,
to do penance, to sin no more,
and to avoid whatever leads me to sin.

Our Saviour Jesus Christ
suffered and died for us.
In his name, my God, have mercy.

The Prayer, My Lord And God

You gave each one of us
a mission to fulfil in our lives.
Help us to find it,
to use it and share it with others.

Help us to understand the true meaning of life,
to know you, and to live with you.

Lord, many a times I stray from your light
and feel that I am not worthy to be called your child,
but I know Lord,
that you are a forgiving Father
and that you accept me as I am.
I know that you love me
like no other can love me,
that your love for me is so great and unconditional
that it hurts me to hurt you.
Help me my Lord,
to become more like you.
Help me to see you in others
and help others see you in me.

A Prayer For World Peace

Lord, we pray for the power to be gentle;
the strength to be forgiving;
the patience to be understanding;
and the endurance to accept the consequences
of holding to what we believe to be right.
May we put our trust in the power of good to
overcome evil
and the power of love to overcome hatred.
We pray for the vision to see and the faith to believe
in a world emancipated from violence,
a new world where fear shall no longer lead men to
commit injustice,

nor selfishness make them bring suffering to others.
Help us to devote our whole life and thought and
energy

to the task of making peace,
praying always for the inspiration and the power
to fulfill the destiny for which we and all men were
created.

Prayer For A Priest

O Jesus, our great High Priest,
Hear my humble prayers on behalf of your priest,
Father .
Give him a deep faith,
a bright and firm hope
and a burning love
which will ever increase in the course of his priestly
life.
In his loneliness,
comfort him In his sorrows,
strengthen him In his frustrations,
point out to him that it is through suffering that the
soul is purified,
and show him that he is needed by the Church,
he is needed by souls,
he is needed for the work of redemption.
O loving Mother Mary,
Mother of Priests,

take to your heart your son
who is close to you because of his priestly
ordination,
and because of the power
which he has received to carry on the work of Christ
in a world which needs him so much.
Be his comfort, be his joy, be his strength,
and especially help him to live
and to defend the ideals of consecrated celibacy.

A Prayer For Moderate Pride

Lord, Your creations display great pride,
Achievements that continually resonate!
Your Divine work luxuriates in eminence;
Your Grandeur leaving me speechless!
Resulting from Your intrinsic sweet nature,
Exalted pride is Yours by legal right.
Endow me with pride for my achievements;
Sheltering me against impious vanity.
May my life mirror spiritual balance,
Respect and satisfaction in my endeavours.
Your Divinity is reflected in all things;
I behold the beauty of Your pride!

Prayer For The Holiness Of Priests.

Grant, O Lord,
that every hand laid upon you at the altar
may be a friendly hand,
whose touch is tender and consoling as Joseph's was;
that the lips which form so many sacred words
may never be profaned by frivolous or unworthy
speech;
that priests may guard,
even in the noisy streets of the city,
the impress of their noble functions,
the bright token that they have
but lately come down from your holy mountain;
and in their garments the fragrance of the altar,
that everyone may find them living memorials of
you,
accessible to all,
yet more than other men.
Grant that they may contract from the Mass of today
a hunger and thirst for the Mass of the morrow,
that the sacred anticipation be their last thought at
night and your tender summons their first awareness
in the morning;
that your priests,
filled with you and your good gifts,
may give largely to the rest of men who look to you.

Prayer For Joyful Priests.

Heavenly Father,
give the Church today
many, holy, prayerful and joyful priests.
May their enthusiasm and good humor
inspire the faithful,
transform our parishes,
extend your Kingdom
and bring you glory.
We pray you through Jesus Christ, your Son.

The Prayer Thank You God!

For all You have given,
Thank You God.
For all You have withheld,
Thank You God.
For all You have withdrawn,
Thank You God.
For all You have permitted,
Thank You God.
For all You have prevented,
Thank You God.
For all You have forgiven me,
Thank You God.
For all You have prepared for me,
Thank You God.

For the death You have chosen for me,
Thank you God.
For the place you are keeping for me in heaven,
Thank You God.
For having created me to love You for eternity,
Thank You God.

The Prayer, A Countyman Gives Thanks

O God, Source and Giver of all things,
who manifests Your infinite majesty,
power and goodness in the earth about us,
we give You honor and glory.

For the sun and rain,
for the manifold fruits of our fields,
for the increase of our herds and flocks,
we thank You.
For the enrichment of our souls with Divine grace,
we are grateful.

Supreme Lord of the harvest,
graciously accept us and the fruits of our toil,
in union with Christ Your Son,
as atonement for our sins,
for the growth of Your Church,
for peace and charity in our homes,
for salvation to all.

A Prayer For World Peace

Lord, we pray for the power to be gentle;
the strength to be forgiving;
the patience to be understanding;
and the endurance to accept the consequences
of holding to what we believe to be right.

May we put our trust in the power of good to
overcome evil
and the power of love to overcome hatred.

We pray for the vision to see and the faith to believe
in a world emancipated from violence,
a new world where fear shall no longer lead men to
commit injustice,
nor selfishness make them bring suffering to others.

Help us to devote our whole life and thought and
energy
to the task of making peace,
praying always for the inspiration and the power
to fulfill the destiny for which we and all men were
created.

Closing Prayer

Lord Jesus Christ,
you were fastened with nails
to the wood of the cross
and raised on high for all to see.
As the sun grew dark and the earth quaked,
you surrendered your spirit to your Father,
descended among the dead,
broke open the gates of hell,
and freed those bound in darkness.
As angel choirs rejoiced,
you were raised to life again on the third day,
destroying death by your own death
and canceling the power of sin.
By these mighty deeds on our behalf,
rescue us from our blindness and tepidity,
inspire us anew by your Holy Spirit,
and lead us into a life of prayer and service
worthy of your awesome sacrifice,
O Savior of the world,
living and reigning with the Father,
in the unity of the Holy Spirit,
one God, for ever and ever.

Printed in Great Britain
by Amazon

48161671R00030